STARTING POINTS

AUTUMN

Ruth Thomson

Photography by Peter Millard

FRANKLIN WATTS
LONDON · NEW YORK · SYDNEY · TORONTO

Franklin Watts Inc.
387 Park Avenue South
New York, NY 10016

Library of Congress Cataloging-in-Publication Data

Thomson, Ruth.
Autumn / by Ruth Thomson.
p.   cm. — (Starting points)
Includes index.
Summary: Provides art and craft projects and activities based on the theme of autumn.
ISBN 0-531-10732-9
1. Autumn—Juvenile literature.   2. Handicraft—Juvenile literature.
[1. Autumn.   2. Handicraft.]   I. Title.   II. Series.
Thomson, Ruth.   Starting points.
QH81.T6112 1989
508—dc20   89-5841   CIP   AC

Editor: Jenny Wood

Design: David Bennett

Typesetting: Typecity

Printed in Belgium

The author and publisher would like to thank Sharon Fuller, Margaret Howker
and members of the Brixton Saturday Explorers Club, in particular Katie Hunt,
Christina Barton and Lucy Mulloy for providing the nature house and the
masks; Amy Williams, Helen Bliss-Williams and Chloe Thomson for their salt
dough models and Leo Thomson for his leaf collage.

Additional photographs:- Aquila: page 19 (top and bottom left)
Biofotos: pages 6 (bottom left), 7 (top and bottom right), 18 (top and left);
Bruce Coleman: pages 6 (bottom left), 8, 9 top left;
Chris Fairclough Color Library: pages 7 (bottom left), 10, 11, 25, 30;
Natural History Picture Agency: page 7 (top right);
Zefa: pages 4, 9 (top right and bottom right and left).

CONTENTS

Autumn Is Here

Leaves fall,
Brown leaves,
Yellow leaves streaked with brown.
They fall,
Flutter,
Fall again.
The brown leaves
And the yellow streaked leaves
Loosen on their branches.
And drift slowly downward.

Amy Lowell

Signs Of Autumn

As the days become shorter and colder, the leaves of deciduous trees start to turn red, orange, yellow or brown and fall off. In spring and summer, the leaves make green chlorophyll, which helps make food for the tree. Without enough sun, the chlorophyll breaks down and the leaves change color.

As the nights become colder, there is more dew each morning. This is the best time to see spiders' webs, which show up with glistening dewdrops on them.

An assortment of different fungi appear in damp woods. Look by the base of trees as well as on old tree stumps and fallen logs to find them.

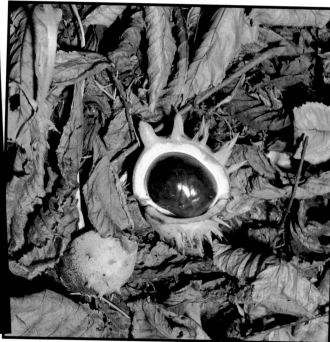

The long-tailed field mouse collects nuts and berries. Sometimes it stores them in an abandoned nest and comes back to feed.

Collect some fallen tree fruits — horse chestnuts in hard, spiky containers, sweet chestnuts in their spiny ones and acorns in their cups.

The fruits of the hedges provide an autumn feast for birds and small mammals. Elderberries hang in clusters.

Wild rose hips, scarlet rowan berries and haws are plentiful. Juicy blackberries grow on thorny brambles.

Animals And Birds

Autumn is a time of change for many animals and birds.

Squirrels, and field mice busily gather stores of food and bury them in holes to use throughout the winter.

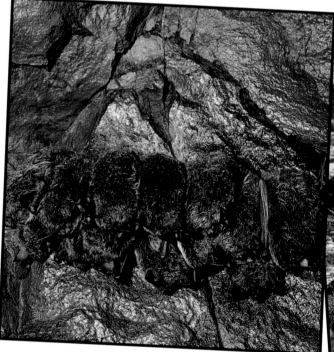

Bats find a sheltered place to spend the winter. Then they go into a sleep called hibernation. Their body temperature drops and their breathing slows down, so they use very little energy.

Deer, foxes and other mammals which stay active all winter grow thicker coats to keep them warm in the cold.

The weasel and the snowshoe rabbit change the color of their coats completely, so they blend with the landscape when winter comes.

Insect-eating birds, such as robins, swallows and thrushes cannot find enough food in winter. They fly thousands of miles to warmer climates and will return in summer. This is called migration.

Birds which breed in the Arctic or in Siberia migrate south in the autumn when there is no longer any food available in the snowy lands of the north.

Collecting Leaves

Broadleaved (deciduous) trees lose their leaves in autumn to protect themselves against cold and water loss.

Collect fallen leaves in parks, on lawns, along the pavements and in the countryside. Keep a notebook of where you find them. Look carefully to find the tree each one has come from. The wind often blows leaves some distance away.

Make notes about the trees. These will help you identify the leaves more easily in a field guide. Note whether the bark is smooth or rough, and what color it is.

Check whether the remaining leaves are arranged on the branches in pairs opposite each other, or alternate singly along each twig. Draw a sketch of the shape of each tree.

Lay the leaves between two sheets of paper — newspaper or blotting paper are best — and put heavy books or bricks on top to press them. Leave the leaves for a week or two to flatten and dry.

Name : Maple
Place : Local park
Leaves : Large leaves with
5 points Dark green,
turning yellow.

Seeds : Pairs of
Winged seeds

Tree shape

Identify Your Leaves

When your leaves are flat and dry, paste them into a scrapbook and label them.

Beech

Birch

English Oak

Basswood

Norway Maple

Black Poplar

Hungarian Oak

Cappadocian Maple

Hawthorn

Red Oak

Alder

Willow

Sweet Chestnut

Mountain Ash (Rowan)

Cherry

Leaf Collages

Use some of your dried leaves to make collage pictures.

This face was made using two sorts of tree fruits as well as leaves. Can you spot which they are?

The fishy shape of these leaves inspired this picture.

You could also use leaves to imitate feathers, scales or hair.

Make an autumn tree. Use a bark rubbing for the trunk. Tape some strong, thin paper over the bark of a tree. Rub the paper with a wax crayon until a pattern appears.

Cut out a trunk shape and paste it on a sheet of paper. Then paste on lots of leaves. How many different kinds can you find on this tree?

Fruits And Seeds

Make a collection of autumn fruits and seeds to compare.

Sweet Chestnuts

Horse Chestnuts

Ornamental Cherries

Maple

By autumn, trees and flowers have developed fruits with seeds inside. A seed contains a tiny plant, called an embryo, and some food to help it start growing. If seeds fell directly under their parent plant, these embryos would not have enough light or moisture to grow. They need to travel as far away as possible to have a chance of growing.

Nuts, cherries and berries are scattered by animals and birds. Alder trees often grow by water. Their seeds float downstream and if they are washed ashore they may start growing.

Broom Pods

Alder 'cones'

Oak acorns

Hawthorn haws

Rosehips

Beech fruits

Plane, ash and birch seeds stay on the tree during winter. The cluster of birch seeds gradually breaks up and the light seeds blow away. The plane seed balls burst open in spring to release their tiny seeds. Ash and maple seeds are in winged cases and are carried by the wind. Pine trees also have winged seeds. These take months to grow their seeds. The cones stay tightly shut while the seeds are growing and when the weather is damp. They open only in dry weather to release their seeds.

Maple Seeds

Ash Keys

Scots Pine Cones

Birch Seeds

Ivy Seeds (unripe)

Seed Dispersal

▲

Maple and ash seeds have wings. On a windy day they spiral and flutter like helicopters, away from the parent tree.

▲

Thistle and dandelion seeds are very light. They have tufts of hair which help them drift far away on the wind.

▲ Broom and other pea-family plants have seeds which grow in pods. The pods stay on the plant. When a pod has dried out, it twists and opens, shooting out the seeds in all directions.

◀ Berries are soft, juicy food for birds, but their seeds are indigestible. Birds eat the fleshy fruit, and the seeds pass out, unharmed, in their droppings.

Burdock grows in hedges. Its seed cases have tiny hooks, which catch on to the fur of passing animals. They may be rubbed off some distance from the plant. ▶

Birds, such as jays, collect and bury acorns and other nuts for the winter. Some they will eat. Those the birds forget may sprout if they are in suitable soil.

Masks

These woodland masks are made of papier mâché and decorated with autumn leaves, cones and feathers.

Things you need:
- **Wallpaper paste**
- **Newspaper torn into strips**
- **Large round balloon**
- **Paints and paintbrushes**
- **Leaves for decoration**

Stand the balloon in a small bowl to keep it upright. Coat the newspaper strips with wallpaper paste. Criss-cross them several layers thick over half the balloon. Smooth down any ends.

Leave the papier mâché to dry for several days. Then remove the balloon. Cut eye, nose and mouth holes in the mask and decorate it. Hold your mask on with elastic, tied round a hole on each side.

Autumn Pictures

Here's an unusual way to display your collection of autumn leaves and fruits.

Cut a yard length of 1″ (2.5 cm) wide wood into either four equal pieces or two long and two shorter pieces. Glue and nail them together into a frame and stain or paint it. Staple your finds on to the back of the frame to make a picture.

If you gather a large collection, you may prefer to display them in a bigger frame like this. Hammer nails, at 2.5 cm (1″) intervals, into the back of it.

Stretch lengths of string at random across the frame and tie the ends round the nails. Weave your finds through the string or tie them on separately.

A Nature House

You could use your finds to make a nature house like this one. The roof is made of twigs, the walls are made of pictures and the floor is soft and leafy.

This house changed all the time as children brought new finds from their walks to tie on.

Autumn Festivals

Autumn is harvest time. Many religions and countries hold festivals in celebration.

Harvest festival

Christians throughout Europe bring gifts of bread, fruit, flowers and vegetables to church for a service of thanksgiving. After the festival, the food is given to old people and others in need.

Thanksgiving

In America, families share a traditional Thanksgiving meal to commemorate the first Thanksgiving which was held by the Pilgrim Fathers, in 1621, to celebrate their first corn harvest.

Succoth

Jewish people celebrate harvest with an eight-day festival called Succoth. They decorate an open-air booth (often a garden shed with the roof removed) with fruit and flowers, and eat festive meals in it all week.

Salt Dough Models

Make some models of trees, fruits, animals and other autumn things.

Recipe for salt dough

Stir together:
- **2 cups plain flour**
- **1 cup salt**
- **1 cup cold water**
- **2 tablespoons cooking oil**

Knead the mixture with your hands until it forms a soft, pliable ball.
Keep your fingertips covered with flour, so that the dough doesn't stick to them.

Coloring the dough

You can use the dough as it is, or you may prefer to color it. Divide it into several balls and add either a few drops of food coloring or paint. (Remember: you can mix food coloring just like paint, to get all sorts of colors.) Knead the dough until the color is well mixed in.

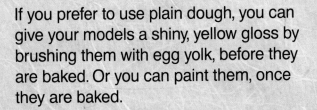

If you prefer to use plain dough, you can give your models a shiny, yellow gloss by brushing them with egg yolk, before they are baked. Or you can paint them, once they are baked.

Line a baking tray with aluminum foil, to provide a non-stick base for your models. Shape the dough as you like and then bake it in the oven at 300°F or 150°C for at least an hour until it is completely hard. The fatter the model, the longer it will take to bake.

Tips and wrinkles

- Put the dough through a garlic squeezer to make strands of hair or prickles.

- Use a knife, a fork and a pastry cutter to give your models texture.

- If you are making a flat model, like this tree or basket, roll out a flat base first and stick the details on with a dab of water.

Grass Figures

On your next autumn walk, collect long, dry grass stems to make some simple figures.

Things you need:

- **Several dozen grass stems soaked in water overnight**
- **Scissors**
- **Strong thread**
- **Felt-tip pens**
- **Fabric scraps**

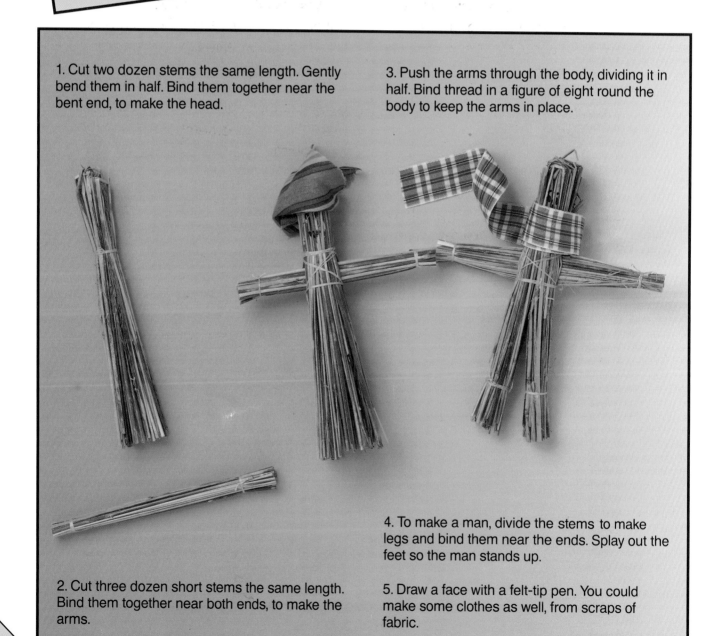

1. Cut two dozen stems the same length. Gently bend them in half. Bind them together near the bent end, to make the head.

2. Cut three dozen short stems the same length. Bind them together near both ends, to make the arms.

3. Push the arms through the body, dividing it in half. Bind thread in a figure of eight round the body to keep the arms in place.

4. To make a man, divide the stems to make legs and bind them near the ends. Splay out the feet so the man stands up.

5. Draw a face with a felt-tip pen. You could make some clothes as well, from scraps of fabric.

More Things To Do

Grow some tree seeds

The seeds that will grow most successfully are beech, oak and horse chestnut. Make sure you choose seeds that are not damaged. Plant several different kinds, so you can compare how they grow.

Put little stones at the bottom of some small flowerpots and fill the pots with moist garden soil. Soak the seeds overnight and put one in each pot, about 2.5 cm (1in) from the top. Fix plastic bags over the pots with string or a large rubber band. This helps keep the soil moist. Stand the pots in a sunny spot and when the seedlings appear, remove the bags and water them regularly. Some seedlings will appear in a few weeks; others may take several months. Be patient!

Bulbs

Plant some indoor bulbs, such as hyacinths, daffodils, tulips and purple crocus in late September or early October.

Use bulb fiber rather than garden soil, because it holds moisture better. Soak the fiber in water and squeeze out any excess. Put a layer at the bottom of a flat-bottomed bowl. Arrange the bulbs quite closely together and cover them with more fiber, leaving just their tips showing. Keep them moist and in the dark. As soon as they begin to grow, put the bowl in a light place. Remember to keep the fiber moist.

Seed pictures

Use flat seeds to make pictures, by sticking them on stiff card. This snail was made of pumpkin seeds, which had first been roasted in an oven to dry.
You could also use ash keys, maple and elm seeds.

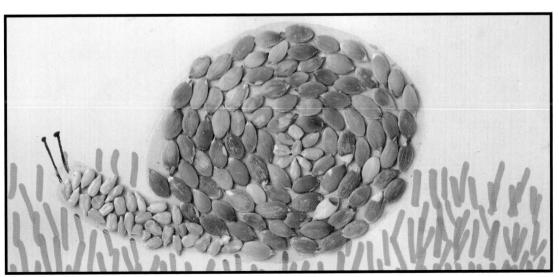

Collect fruits and seeds

Collect a variety of fruits and seeds from trees, shrubs and flowers and put them into groups, according to the way they travel.

• Winged seeds

These include ash, maple, basswood, pine and fir.

See how far seeds with one wing travel compared with those with two wings. Throw the seeds up in the air and measure how far they travel. Try doing this first indoors and then on a windy day outdoors. Notice the difference in the way they move.

• Edible seeds

These include nuts such as acorns, hazelnuts, beech nuts and horse chestnuts, and berries such as blackberry, ivy, holly, rose hip, juniper, dogwood and elderberry.
Remember: **Never eat wild berries** unless an adult tells you they are safe. Birds and animals can eat berries which are poisonous for people.

Make notes about how the seeds are protected and say whether there is one or more seed in each fruit.

• Plumed seeds

These include dandelion, thistle, birch, willow and poplar.

Blow a plumed seed head and watch how the seeds scatter and are caught on the air currents. They can travel for several miles.

• Seeds with exploding pods

These include poppy, false acacia and honesty. **Never try to eat any of these seeds; they are poisonous.**

• Hooked fruits

These include agrimony, stick seed and burdock.

See what these fruits will cling to. Try them on wood, plastic, wool, cotton, fur, metal and artificial fibers, such as nylon or rayon. Notice if it is difficult to remove them from any particular sort of texture.

An autumn quiz

1. Which of these trees have winged seeds?
   a) oak   b) ash   c) beech
   d) maple   e) horse chestnut

2. Which of these animals hibernate for the winter?
   a) fox   b) bat   c) squirrel
   d) rabbit   e) chipmunk   f) deer

3. Which of these birds migrate in autumn?
   a) house martin   b) cuckoo
   c) swallow   d) turtle dove   e) swift

4. Which of these fruits is the odd one out?
   a) beechnut   b) haw   c) acorn
   d) elderberry   e) ash key

5. When do pine cones open to release their seeds?
   a) in dry weather
   b) in wet weather
   c) in cold weather

6. What is a deciduous tree?
   a) a tree that keeps its leaves all year round
   b) a tree that loses its leaves in autumn
   c) a tree that flowers in winter

7. What is the fruit of a conifer called?
   a) a nut   b) a cone   c) a berry
   d) a hip

Autumn words

How would you describe autumn? Think about the colors, atmosphere, sights, weather and your feelings. Here are some words to start you thinking.

Colors		Weather		Nature	
tint	streaked	showery	drizzle	flutter	gleam
hue	pallor	blustery	frosty	whirl	bloom
golden		breezy	crisp	hide	migrate
amber		bright		wither	disperse
bronze		nippy		bare	quiver
tawny		dull		scatter	twirl
tinge		dim		drift	mellow
russet		misty		ripe	glimmer
crimson		cheery		glisten	shrivel
scarlet		gusty		gather	wilt
rosy		dank		harvest	crunchy
burnished		moist		store	

Index

Answers to the autumn quiz

1. Ash and maple have winged seeds.

2. The bat and the chipmunk hibernate for the winter.

3. All these birds migrate in autumn.

4. The ash key is the odd one out. It is the only seed that is not edible.

5. Pine cones open to release their seeds in dry weather.

6. A deciduous tree is one that loses its leaves in autumn.

7. The fruit of a conifer is called a cone.